AN INTRODUCTION TO NAPLES' POSTCOLONIAL LEGACY.

ON LUCHÈ AND CO'SANG

VKY

Editions Canaan

In loving memory of André and Paula
Kabeya.

Introduction

This book represents the introduction and first part of a second and longer thesis surrounding CO'SANG and LUNATIC through a comparative study of the lyrics and music of the two legendary groups on a political, social and cultural aspect of their respective work in both France and Italy.

Though Italy remains present and active in the European political scene, the history of the country is still rarely explored in the rest of the world except for the impact the Renaissance had in Europe.

What can be said about colonialism? There again, the failure of the Italian armies in Ethiopia are barely mentionned elsewhere and the troubled passage of the Reunification even less.

This introduction mostly focuses on the modern history of Naples, the colonial war which was known as *Risorgimento* and its heritage through the discouse of Luchè and his former band, Co'Sang. If Italian rap has become more recognized over the last few years with the help of Sfera Ebbasta among others, the scene was always rich and diverse. Centered around Milan, Bologna and Naples, many acts became popular within the underground movements and never truly reached the international level of fame.

This short analysis focuses on one of the most important groups of the 1990s and 2000s and one of his leaders, Luchè.

Born Luca Imprudente in 1981, the rapper grew up in Marianella, one of the most dangerous and poorest ghettos dominated by the Mafia and rhythmed by criminal activities. If French artists from the new generation such as SCH, PNL or SADEK, encouraged by the glamourization of Gomorra, candidly shot their videos in Scampia to gain more street credibility, the ghetto was mostly unknown to strangers before. And so was Neapolitan rap.

In this struggle, the legacy of CO'SANG seems to have weakened over the years. Luchè and Nto, without or within the collective, represented more than a simple rap band. Their «avant-garde» and lyrical approach was a reminiscence of a legitimate Mobb Deep influence, highlighted by the crude and dark tales of the two young men who witnessed the madness of their society. They were not only musicians but a living testimony of Naples by rapping in dialect. This book takes a look at the heritage of Italy's colonial past through the eyes of the artist. Though not political in any form, Luchè has always proven to be musically consistent and well aware of the social and political structure that made him.

No clash, diss and personal anecdotes related to the motives behind the separation of CO'SANG will be brought to attention.

Get the Italian version on Editions Canaan.

By the mid to the late 1990s, the Western European hip-hop scene has darkened and became way more political. Co'Sang, like Lunatic or La Mafia K1Fry in France contributed to the emergence of a dialogue evolving around the issue of colonialism. In France, hip-hop is dominated by the second generation of immigrants whose members belong to the social and identity fracture. There, one can distinguish two waves. On the one hand, one can mention the mainstream success of collectives and groups such as Secteur Ä. Though criticized for their social origin, their hip-hop is exposed to a wider audience with the exception of 2BAL or Arsenik, pioneers in hardcore rap, Lino having established the foundations of modern French rap. This mainstream form of rap is opposed to a more underground and censored rap scene. Deemed too realistic and violent, the artists are not played in radios. The late 1990s was marked by debates concerning colonialism and slavery. In May 1998, in Paris, a march reunited 40,000 peaceful protestors for the recognition of slavery as a crime against humanity. At the time, the far right party Front National is present and racist crimes are on the rise in Paris and Marseille. In 1995, rap became more political. Formed in 1997, Co'Sang belongs to the underground Italian scene and is not mainstream at all. The band is political in essence and way more crude.

Co'Sang was, therefore, one of the earliest political acts in Italian rap history for they represented the essence of the dehumanized Neapolitan man made to be ashamed of his condition. The affirmation of their identity was a rebellious act that defied unfair prejudices which were born centuries ago. The two men refused to bow down and would rather amplify their heritage by rapping in dialect.

In France, the Mafia K1 Fry, around the same period in the late 1990s, had to deal with censorship for the violence of their lyrics. Actually, the Mafia was one of the first supergroups of the second wave whose young rappers understood the complexity of their condition as children of the ghetto. With songs like *HARD CORE* by Ideal J, the members knew their social condition was the direct result of colonialism. If nationally played, the collective could have encouraged other young citizens of the ghetto to revolt. Though imperfect in their manner and trapped in their own contradictions, the Mafia K1 Fry was a turning point. Other bands such as Expression Direkt followed the same pattern.

Co'Sang did not need to point out anything and did not have to lean back to analyze their experience. They already embodied the fatality of their colonial past. In this sense, Co'Sang would be more similar to Lunatic, reflecting the consciousness of Ali and the darkness of Booba, both groups sharing the same

13

influence in Mobb Deep. Yet, the Neapolitans had the more authentic experience when it came to violence. If members of the Mafia K1 Fry were executed in gang fights, and if Booba and Ali grew up in destitution along with the Mafia K1 Fry, the experience of Nto and Luchè was the ultimate fantasy of the others. Italian crime was always seen as the epitome of a street lifestyle with names such as Mafia K1 Fry which illustrate our point. Many Lunatic songs at the time made reference to the Sicilian Cosa Nostra and the mafia lifestyle in general.

If wars in Africa are openly linked to colonialism, conflicts in the Middle East, Asia or Latin America are put on the account of a bad political management from the presidents themselves. Yet, colonialism per se is way too often associated with «people of color», a factor proper to inhabitants of the Third World. This conception in itself is incomplete for history has proven many times that colonialism does not only apply to Africans. A few Europeans have, unfortunately, been dehumanized, victims of racism, isolation and submitted to inhumane treatments. However, due to their European identity and geographic origin, their trauma were never counted as part of a colonial agenda.

If the late ex president of Burkina Faso, Thomas Sankara, once made a point about Europeans exploiting their own before taking advantage of Africans, it is falsely believed that Europeans were always strangers to abuse. The conflicts in the Balkans or the Troubles in Northern Ireland are one of a few examples. Italy was not exempted neither. Still, the brutality of the recent events of the country were presented as simple invasions involving several peoples.

Risorgimento and Dehumanization of the Neapolitans

Luchè is the human and artistic extension of a people affected by the horrifc legacy of the Risorgimento and has alluded to the dehumanization of his ancestors. Through his discourse, he places himself as a post-colonial subject submitted to diverse afflictions which flew from a colonial and brutal past. The Reunification of Italy, known as *Risorgimento,* was a political and social movement which sealed the modern identity of Italy. Celebrated as one of the most progressive historic events at a time, the leaders having been inspired by the 1789 French Revolution, the process began in 1848 and finished in 1871, when Rome became the capital.

Before the first waves of rebellion broke off, Italy as we know it today was made of different kingdoms whose citizens had their own culture and dialects.

The Reunification did lead to a cultural enrichment of the people but it was above all, dominated by its brutal nature. Indeed, the *Risorgimento* was accompanied by a colonial territorial war symbolized by the Expedition of the Thousand (*Spedizione dei Mille*). Giuseppe Garibaldi, a former exiled fighter from North Italy who lived in Argentina for many years before returning to Italy, supported by a thousand men, left Quarto near Genoa and went to Sicily where they overthrew the Kingdom of the Two Sicilies. Though hailed as a fascinating chapter in modern history, the actions of Garibaldi were the apex of a colonial war between Northern Italian forces represented by the Kingdom of Savoy and a destroyed Kingdom of the Two Sicilies.

The Reunification was never meant to reunite and share profits equally between citizens living in the same territory but the realization of a planned scheme aiming at invading the Southern part of Italy for financial issues. Riddled with debts after many wars against Austria during the French occupation of the Northern region, the House of Savoy, with the help of the United Kingdom, the United States, France and the Canadian freemasonry decided to invade the prosperous Two Sicilies. Ahead of its time and well developped in terms of infrastructures, King Ferdinand II had to pay the price for having decided to remain neutral during the French Revolutionary Wars against Prussia. The ports of the Two Sicilies represented a strategic point for the belligerents. Yet, they were met with the refusal of the Sicilian King. Contrary to his neighbours whom leaders had put an emphasis on protecting and supporting the army, the King of the Two Sicilies had rather relied on the development of infrastructures believing neutrality would be an eternal benefit. This decision cloistered the kingdom even more from international life. Garibaldi was thus armed by foreign forces and managed to overthrow the stability of Southern Italy. The House of

Savoy had interests in the war. Indeed, using Garibaldi was the ultimate way to plunder the resources of the Two Sicilies. The war left an imprint on the Southern population for centuries and somehow shaped their discourse. Due to years of political invasions, the citizen of the Two Sicilies became a subject of hatred and mockery for the Northerners.

Co'Sang has the ultimate street experience which surpasses the madness in France. The degree of violence they face on a daily basis is more problematic and shocking than the one of the Mafia K1 Fry. The two Neapolitans are strangers to living a life of fantasy for they live in a lost area dominated by the Mafia which involves the proliferation of baby killers, a tale almost non-existent in French hip-hop. In this sense, Co'Sang is more of a Mobb Deep reflection for the two collectives share the same form of destitution and the same degree of ferocity glamourized by Hollywood and hailed in many American rap songs. Yet, one faces a limit. If Mobb Deep are an American duo, their vision as Black men in the United States differs from Lunatic's. Therefore, Booba and Ali are closer to Luchè and Nto for they truly reflect each other's voices in a post-colonial society. Their music highlights the loss of a glorious past which was taken away from them due to colonialism. Both Co'Sang and Lunatic were the product of historic brutality which weakened and crushed them. Their discourse is met with disdain and they are perceived as low individuals, condemned and crucified by the fate of history.

Born Luca Imprudente in 1981, Luchè is a Neapolitan rapper and former member of legendary group Co'Sang, along with Nto. Though pioneers in Neapolitan rap and highly innovative in terms of artistry, writing and composition, Luchè and Nto both have had a prolific career ever since they separated. However, few have managed to enlighten the importance of their speech in Italy's post-colonial past and context. This period of history is rather belittled by the official theory. If colonial studies have been at the forefront for a few years now, they mostly focus on African issues.

In a Western sphere where race has become a trending topic, Africa has over overshadowed the other parts of the world where European entities have submitted other White peoples. At the time of his discourse, Luchè is already dehumanized by the fate of history. Though European and White, he belongs to the lowest rank of Whiteness. He is a White man, destroyed by colonial history who also inherits from the horrible legacy of racial theories from the early 20th century. If Africans face a harsh treatment, it is often forgotten to precise that these theories were first applied and tested against other groups of White people deemed inferior. In this sense, Luchè is alienated from this particular heritage.

He is a post-colonial subject whose ancestors have been deprived from enjoying the status of human beings.

By the early 20th century, racist theoricians such as Madison Grant began to influence American politics in the establishment of racist ideas. Obviously, these ideologies evolved around the superiority of a White Northern European race which would dominate the world and Third World populations. Their genes would grant them spiritual, mental and physical superiority over the others. Yet, according to these racist ideas, the racists truly want to make a distinction within the White race. There again, the Northern race dominates the Southern one whose citizens are not recognized as pure in their Whiteness. Indeed, the racists judged the Northerners to be the guardians of racial purity while the Southerners were not. Due to centuries of Moorish presence in the region, the Southerners are seen as mixed-race individuals and thus worthy of disdain. Modern Spaniards, Southern Italians and Portuguese are, until this day, labeled as sub-Whites. In Italy, the Reunification somehow preceded the expansion of racial theories from the early 20th century promoted by Madison Grant but it sealed the racial ideologies when it came to the alleged lower position of the Southerners. With the fall of the Two Sicilies came the destitution of the Southern Italian. After the kingdom was overthrown, the Northern Italian forces took pleasure in molesting, torturing and deporting the Southerners. The devaluation of their status carried on under the regime of Benito Mussolini, a time when any young Southern man suspected of criminal activity was badly tortured and sentenced to prison. The political and social disdain for the Neapolitan starts there. He wears the scars left by centuries of scientific racist theories. Considered the father of Modern science in Italy, Cesare Lombroso was responsible for the proliferation of these racist theories in the Nation. A fervent supporter of the invasion, the Jewish-Italian scientist «contended that the born criminal could be detected by certain physical caracteristics such as high cheekbones and upturned noses»(1).

Lombroso did not stop there and went further. For the sake of scientific progress, he studied and measured the skulls of Southern prisoners to justify their alleged criminal nature. By using sciences and sociological factors, the Southern Italian was broken once again in all aspects. The scheme used by the Savoy forces was no different from the tactics of the Belgians or the French during the colonial era in Africa. The plundering of the land was always justified by a process of destruction of the people.

Sporco Napoletano

The demise of Luchè lies in the hypocrisy of Italian history. The explosion of criminal activities in the region is not the result of a supposed natural criminal essence which would be attached to Southern Italians only. It is due to the political decline of the Two Sicilies. The revolution destabilized and prevented the region from further expansion and growth. The exclusion of the Neapolitans, victims of racism from Northern Italians today is a reflection of colonialism and its stigma. The children of the periphery or ghettos such as Marianella, from where the members of Co'Sang came from, are even more exposed to prejudices for being poor. Both French and Italian authorities

29

try to change their narrative by separating the consequences of colonialism from the ghetto experience, in an attempt to blame the subjects for their own poverty, in an order to belittle their discourse.

However, Naples stands out in the post-colonial context. The Neapolitans do not remain silent and take pride in their heritage, even if history made them weak to the eyes of the world. The Neapolitan speaks up and never bows down.

«Lo faccio soló per la mia città»
Luchè, Per la Mia Città, Malammore, 2016

Luchè's *Per la Mia Città* highlights a real separation between Naples and Italy. Naples is not Italy. The town is opposed to the rest of the Nation. This detail reveals that the spectrum of the Reunification is still well alive in the minds of the citizens. Some individuals do not feel like they belong to any form of oneness. The people from Marianella evolve in the sphere of the banished, where death reigns. This fatality is not only caused by the brutality of the Mafia but by the psychological and mental desperation of the population.

The spectrum of colonialism in Italy alienates the Neapolitans more than the French immigrants in the ghetto. Though excluded in their own periphery, France is not torn apart by territorial disparities for the Nation is unified. The rejection of Naples by the Italian authorities make the isolation even harder and humiliating. It favors a reclusion for the inhabitants of the ghettos in Naples. There lies the importance of self-affirmation of one's heritage, the representation of Neapolitan roots and the transmission of Neapolitan culture. It is through the valorisation of themselves that Luchè finds the ultimate response against years of historic brutatily, without being a political rapper himself.

The artist always makes sure to mention other important Neapolitican political figures such as Nino D'Angelo, Pino Daniele or Massimo Troisi, using his artistic platform to give value to the destroyed and shamed. Naples and its ghettos are the extension of the troubles caused by the Reunification as we said earlier. Consequently, Luchè in both his solo career and during the Co'Sang era, is aware of his background and stands proud in representing Naples and defending his people against any attack. He belongs to the oppressed. When not praising Neapolitan icons, Luchè openly refers to Malcolm X, reinforcing the postcolonial context of his work and proving once more that he does not see himself as being apart of the privileged. Growing up in a hostile environment where his kind is not welcome, the experience of Luchè resonates among African-Americans and in the United States where crime is disproportionate.

In his texts, the image of Malcolm X changes and the leader is no longer the voice of the oppressed of the Blacks but to the disadvantaged worldwide, whether Black or White. This detail thus consolidates the ideology of colonialism being universal.

Resistance by language

Luchè clearly finds his extension among the African-American community. His constant references to Malcolm X illustrates our point. Having grown up in a hostile environment where his kind was not welcome, the experience of Luchè resonates among African-Americans and in the United States where crime is disproportionate. In his texts, the image of Malcolm X changes and the leader is no longer the voice of the oppressed of the Blacks but of the disadvantaged worldwide, whether Black or White. This detail thus consolidates the ideology of colonialism being universal. Therefore, due to the troubled history of Naples and the social isolation of his city, a parellel can be made between the two communities. This eventually highlights the brutal theories promoted by the racists who referred to Southern Europeans as the «Negroes of Europe».

The condition of Luchè can not be compared to the one of the French-African immigrants for France is a unified country having a different view on the treatment of its immigrants. Even if racism does exist with Africans being the victims of police brutality, the life in the ghetto is dangerous in some parts but still the violence is limited. In this sense, the inhabitants of Marianella share the same life experience when it comes to the treatment of violence. In both regions, it is disproportionate and involve the use of children to commit the most despicable actions.

The French-African immigrant left his country for France. He is thus a foreign entity who recently came to a new Nation and who deals with rejection. He mostly has to deal with the feeling of xenophobia along with racism. Luchè, like any Neapolitan of his social class is pushed aside on his own land and is not an immigrant. The nature of his discrimination is close to the African-American condition. The Black Americans were once foreigners, it is true, yet they gradually became American citizens and were never given the right to be recognized as such for the color of their skin. They were, therefore, segregated on their own land, where they have been living for more than four hundread years. In both cases, the two categories find the root of the creation of their ghettos in segregation and colonialism.

With the constant mention of Malcolm X, Luchè clearly identifies himself as a colonized individual crucified by the brutality of history. As a colonized man or White European man evolving in a postcolonial sphere, language is used as a powerful tool of resistance, in both solo and group career, Co'Sang being the initiator of a movement. Indeed, both Luchè and Nto, after their separation, kept rapping in dialect before singing in academic Italian, even if Luchè was raised by two intellectual parents who barely spoke in dialect at home(2). This act is not a provocation but rather a political action to fight against the depreciation of Neapolitan identity and as a way to resist the colonial imprint. By rapping in their native language, the men assert their pride in their heritage. A language is a symbol of power for any population and by imposing the most academic form of Italian, one despises the rich heritage of Neapolitan culture. The language is perceived by the authorities as dirty and made for the stupid and poor. Still, both Nto and Luchè gave a new space to their native language in order to narrate their life experience like few others before. The official idiom is linked to authority and thus to the state. Imposing it to the rest of the Italian territory is a vivid memory of the fact that the Reunification was never a collective movement but the application of a plan by force. Speaking in dialect allows Luchè to navigate through the duality of a reality. Naples comes before Italy.

Through his speech, Luchè is already a part of the excluded, belonging to the poor and rejected. His words are those a dispossessed human and can not be marketed to the eyes of the dominant. The use of dialect is subtle and open it to a wider audience whose listeners are not always familiar with Neapolitan culture. This language is not only his but it also represents the people of his condition who have been pushed aside from society. The use of dialect helps Luchè to reappropriate his space. Indeed, by rapping in his native tongue with so much ease and technique, he is the only narrator of his life and no one selse could take this away from him. He would not let any one deny his reality and the use of the dialect questions the power of the State and its legitimacy. Which voice should be more important in the discourse? Would it be the colonizer's or the colonized entity's?

The question of language is no more different than the one which refers to the wave of dub poets in Jamaica in the 1970s and 1980s. At the time, the artists rejected academic English as a sign of education and would rather speak and sing in patois. Mikey Smith (1954-1983) was one of the first legends of the movement as the poem *Mi Cyan Believe It* shows it. Sang in patois , the title, a deformation of *I Can't Believe It* testifies of a real desire of self-appropriation of one's discourse and narration. The problem of Neapolitan dialogue enlightens the hypocrisy which lies behind the choice of the critieria laying the foundation when it comes to the valuation of a culture. That one is always related to marketability and not to the legitimacy of history. The respect and appreciation of it always depend on the capitalization of the language spoken. Contrary to the destructuration of the French language in the ghetto, done on purpose by the inhabitants of the ghetto, Neapolitan on the other hand is the manifestation of the soul of a people and therefore can not be despised or qualified. It is an essence. The essence of the oppressed.

CONCLUSION

Even if Luchè is not a political artist, his rap is not only musical but the historic testimony from the point of view of a Neapolitan man. He uses references to Black political figures such as Malcolm X and is well aware of the importance in the cultural transmission of Neapolitan culture. The rapper does not hesitate to use the racist insults said against Southern Italians, especially Neapolitans, such as «Sporco Napoletano» (Dirty Neapolitan) a derogatory word of abuse used by members of the Lega Nord, the far right Italian party.

If French-Italian rapper Akhenaton who also collaborated with Co'Sang in the past has written about the condition of Neapolitans following the history of colonialism in songs such as *PAESE* from the 2001 album *SOL INVICTUS*, the I AM leader mostly wrote from the point of view of the son of Italian immigrants in Marseille, where Luchè opens up in the most agressive way. This dialogue confirms how colonialism can affect any individual, even though White and European in origin. The next publication will focus on a comparative study between the bands Lunatic and Co'Sang and their impact on the post-colonial context. The work will be published in the year 2021.

SOURCES AND LIST OF BOOKS CONSULTED

ARTICLES

Craniums, Criminals and the 'Cursed Race': Italian Anthropology in American Racial Thought, 1861-1924. by Peter D'Agostino in Comparative Studies in Society and History, Vol 44, n°2 (April 2002) pp. 319-343, Published by Cambridge University Press (1)

«*Fantastically Wrong: The Scientist who seriously believed criminals were part Ape*», WIRED Magazine, by MATT SIMON, 11.12.14

«RACE, STATISTICS AND ITALIAN EUGENICS: ALFREDO NICEFORO'S TRAJECTORY FROM LOMBROSO TO FASCISM (1876-1960)» by Angelo Matteo Caglioti, July 3rd 2017, in SAGE JOURNALS

*«The Racist Theory behind facial recognition»*by SHAKIL CHINOY, The New York Times, July 10th, 2019

BOOKS

MAFIAS. L'INDUSTRIE DE LA PEUR, De Saint Victor, Jacques, Monaco editions du Rocher, 2008

UN POUVOIR INVISIBLE; LES MAFIAS ET LA SOCIÉTÉ DÉMOCRATIQUE (XIXè-XXème), De Saint Victor, Jacques, Gallimard,Paris

IL GOLPE INGLESE, Fasanella, Giovanni, Cereghino, Mario José, Chiarelettere, 2011

LA NAZIONE NAPOLETANA, Controstorie borboniche e identià suddista, DI Fiore Gigi, Utet Libri, 2015

CONTROSTORIA DELL'UNITAD'ITALIA: Fatti e Misfatti del Risorgimento, Di Fiore, Gigi, Rizzoli, 2010

1861- LA STORIA DEL RISORGIMENTO CHE NON C'E SUI LIBRI DI STORIA, Fasanella, Giovanni, Grippo Antonella, editions SPERLING AND KUPFER, 2010

GLI STATI UNITI E IL RISORGIMENTO D'ITALIA 1848-1901, Fiorentino, Daniele, Editore Gangemi, 2014

IL GIORNO DOPO, Luchè, Rizzoli, 2019 (2)

THE PASSING OF THE GREAT RACE, Grant, Madison, Editions Lulu, 1916, 2011 (new edition)

RE-IMAGINING DEMOCRACY IN THE MEDITERANNEAN 1780-1860 edited by Innes, Joanna and Philip, Mark, Oxford University Press, 2018

BOOBA: ANALYSE D'UN DISCOURS POST-COLONIAL 1995-2017, VKY, Editions Canaan, 2018, deuxième édition Juin 2020.